10

W0114406

THE OPEN MEDIA PAMPHLET SERIES

THE OPEN MEDIA PAMPHLET SERIES

TO ORDER ADDITIONAL SERIES TITLES CALL 1 (800) 596-7437

THE OPEN MEDIA PAMPHLET SERIES

Microradio & Democracy

(LOW) POWER TO THE PEOPLE

GREG RUGGIERO

Series editors Greg Ruggiero and Stuart Sahulka

SEVEN STORIES PRESS / New York

Earlier versions of *Microradio & Democracy* originally
appeared in *Z* magazine, *Project Censored Newsletter*,
Chicago Media Watch Newsletter, and *LIP Magazine*.

A Seven Stories Press First Edition,
published in association with Open Media.

Open Media Pamphlet Series editors,
Greg Ruggiero and Stuart Sahulka.

Library of Congress Cataloging-in-Publication Data

Ruggiero, Greg.
    Microradio & Democracy / Greg Ruggiero.
    p. cm. —(The Open Media Pamphlet Series #10)
    ISBN 1-58322-000-3 (pbk.)
    1. Pirate radio broadcasting—United States. 2.
Pirate radio broadcasting—Government policy—United
States. I. Title. II. Series.
HE8697.65 U6R84 1999
384.54'0973—dc21   99-11326
                                         CIP

Book design by Cindy LaBreacht

9 8 7 6 5 4 3 2 1

Printed in the U.S.A.

If there is no struggle, there
is no progress.

Those who profess freedom and
yet deprecate agitation are men
who want crops without plowing
up the ground. They want the rain
without thunder and lightning.
They want the ocean without the
awful roar of its many waters.

This struggle may be a moral one;
or it may be a physical one; or it
may be both moral and physical;
but it must be a struggle.

Power concedes nothing without
a demand.

—FREDERICK DOUGLASS

Special thanks for feedback, ideas, criticism and support: Robert Perry, Peter Franck, Robert W. McChesney, Barbara Olshansky & The Center for Constitutional Rights, Dan Simon & Seven Stories Press, Jessica Glass, Mike Eisenmenger, Carlos Pareja, Paper Tiger Television Collective, Stephen Provizer, Kate Duncan, Flora Martins, Pete tri Dish, Sara Zia Ebrahimi, Diane Fleming, David Murphy, DJ Chrome, Ciani Mendez, Jesse Hirsch, Tamara Ford, Eric Galatas, Jay Sand, Stephen Dunifer, Lynn Gerry, Danny Schechter, Michael Manekin, Crystal and the National Commission for Democracy in Mexico, and all the radio rebels at Steal This Radio 88.7fm.

CONTENTS

FOREWORD

by Robert W. McChesney

A stunning transformation has overwhelmed and reconstructed U.S. radio broadcasting in the past few years. Since 1996 nearly one-half of the 11,000 commercial radio stations have been sold, almost always by smaller firms to medium sized firms, by medium sized firms to larger firms, and by large chains to a few massive powers that own hundreds of stations. At the top of the heap these few giants control some one-third of the market. With companies permitted to own up to eight stations in a single market, most U.S. communities find that their numerous radio stations are in fact owned predominantly by two or three firms.

This transformation of U.S. radio points to the absurdity of the notion that commercial broadcasting "gives the people what they want." In fact this market power gives the radio giants the power to give the people whatever they can make the most profit from. So it is, across the United States, the new radio chains slash costs by reducing staff. After all, one technician or news reporter can service all eight of a firm's stations in a market. And the radio giants use their holdings to better craft a product to serve advertisers, the people they really do try to "give what they want." Hence radio is a leading element in the commercial carpetbombing of our society.

The situation is thick with irony. Radio is the least expensive electronic medium to use as a consumer. It is also quite inexpensive to produce quality fare for broadcast. It is, therefore, ideal for being a community based medium. At the hands of the radio giants, however, radio has become arguably the most centralized and regimented of our mass media. When a company owns rock stations in 50 markets, for example, it hardly needs music directors in 50 markets making extensive contacts with the local community. One playlist, sent from national headquarters, is much less expensive and easier to coordinate with national advertising sales.

The investment community is ecstatic about the massive profits these huge radio combines can generate; but there is no evidence that these profits are due to improved radio programming. Quite the contrary. Without wishing to romanticize the earlier age of radio, whatever semblance of radio being a creative medium, or a local medium, has pretty much been eliminated. Radio today has all the charm of a second-tier suburban shopping mall, if that. Sadly, public broadcasting, meaning for the most part the system of stations associated with National Public Radio, has been unable to fill the void. Encouraged to go commercial themselves, the public stations are kept on a short leash by the political right and have accepted a niche of serving a sliver of the upper-middle class with conventional news and classical music. It is a service decidedly of no interest to the bulk of Americans.

The nature of U.S. radio today also reveals the silliness of the notion that this brand of commercial broadcasting is the "natural" American system. There is nothing natural about it; it is the result of corrupt federal policies rammed through in almost complete secrecy by powerful lobbies. As a result, the commercial broadcasters receive licenses to broadcast on scarce

GREG RUGGIERO

publicly owned frequencies at no charge, a gift from the taxpayers to corporate America valued in the tens of billions of dollars. When Congress relaxed the ownership requirements in 1996 so companies could own eight stations in a single market, there was not a shred of public coverage or debate over the issue.

In theory, the role of the Federal Communications Commission is to regulate commercial broadcasters so they will perform in the "public interest." In fact, the FCC's main function has been and is to guarantee the broadcasters maximum profits. When FCC Chair Bill Kennard had the temerity to suggest that there might be too much concentration in radio ownership in 1998, the commercial broadcasters had their stooges in Congress tell Kennard to back down, or face the elimination of FCC funding. He backed down.

Which brings us to microradio broadcasting. This is an extraordinary and extremely inexpensive technology that offers the promise of opening up a whole new sector of community broadcasting, for people who are not billionaires and whose goal is not to simply turn listeners upside down and shake all the money out of their pockets. This is a rare opportunity to provide a truly democratic layer of broadcasting, without interfering with the signals of any of the existing broadcasters. Yet the commercial broadcasters oppose microradio broadcasting, because they fear competition. And bureaucrats tend to fear microradio broadcasting, unless they can use it to build up political capital.

But microradio is here, and it can no longer be repressed. The question now is what type of microradio broadcasting will be authorized by the FCC. Greg Ruggiero has done a mighty service by explaining the issues of microradio broadcasting and outlining the crucial struggle that is taking place at this very moment in

Washington, DC. Whether microradio is open to all and aims to serve local communities, or whether microradio's function will be to provide another tier of commercial broadcasting hangs in the balance. Microradio is not "the answer" to all of our media problems, but it can be an important first step in the process of making our media accountable to Main Street, rather than to Wall Street and Madison Avenue. Read this pamphlet, share it with your friends, and get active. If popular support for noncommercial, community-based microradio emerges, this is a fight we can and will win.

Urbana, Illinois
March 25, 1999

GREG RUGGIERO

MICRORADIO & DEMOCRACY

(LOW) POWER TO THE PEOPLE*

Based on notes prepared for a presentation given at the Festival of Resistance organized by the NY Zapatistas, NYC, October 12, 1998.

Where there is even a pretense of democracy," writes Noam Chomsky, "communications are at its heart." Given the present state of our society however, it's no surprise that we find communications not at the heart of a vibrant democracy, but rather in the grip of an oppressive and contradictory system of mass control. Nowhere is this more evident than in the struggle for community access to the airwaves and the corporate/government campaign to crush it. The purpose of this pamphlet is to spread news about the free radio movement—about how winning access to the airwaves will provide an advantage in the battle to defend public spaces and civic powers from further downsizing by business interests—an advantage much needed in the larger liberation struggle being waged here and around the world.

To begin building a better world, we must first achieve democracy—the process by which whole communities may meaningfully participate in decision making. And to make intelligent, well formed decisions, we must be able to receive, produce, debate, and share information openly and freely. It is for this reason that a public access media system is a non-negotiable demand in the struggle for democratic society.

Democracy depends on public spaces and public fora, because it is precisely there that we have the power to exercise our rights and freedoms. The founders of this country envisioned a pluralistic society where every citizen's right to communicate would be protected, not squelched, by the government. In today's electronic era, however, speech limited to street corner shouting and leafleting is a miserably disadvantaged way to communicate with one's community. For democratic society to exist, to exercise speech in the ways meant by the framers of the Constitution, communities must have access to the town square of the information age—the airwaves—itself public property, and thus a space where our free speech should be fully exercised and protected. But this is not the case.

COMMERCIALISM AND CIVIL SOCIETY

The problem is commercialism—the unrelenting forces that shape society according to the conditions most

COPS DESCEND ON MICRORADIO ACTIVISTS, DUPONT CIRCLE, WASHINGTON, DC, OCTOBER 5, 1998.

GREG RUGGIERO

favorable to business. Almost every aspect of our lives—
our work, food, housing, education, and culture—is dominated by the pro-business mission of commercialism.
In our present age, business is defined by massive corporations. Commercial influence on law—deregulation—has been to permit corporations to merge into new
monolithic entities that control more economic and
political power than many of the earth's countries.
Indeed, commercial corporations, not nation-states, are
emerging as the new global superpowers—and their goal
as businesses is to make the most possible amount of
money in the shortest possible time, regardless of the
human or ecological consequences.

U.S. COMMUNICATIONS HISTORY

Nowhere have U.S. citizens lost greater control of their
public sphere than in the government's mismanagement
of the airwaves. To study the history of radio policy in
this country is to study how business interests gradu-
ally gain control over a priceless public resource without benefitting civil society. Understanding how our
society can suffer such blows while still claiming to be
a democracy is well worth considering, and may even
suggest tactics to reverse the trend.

Radio was introduced to the Western world by
Guglielmo Marconi in 1895. By 1907 interest in the technology had reached the general population, and by 1912
hundreds of pioneers began broadcasting in the United
States. In August of that year Congress passed the Radio
Act of 1912, which required all broadcasters to first
acquire a license.

Under the Radio Act of 1912, noncommercial radio
flourished. Tens of thousands of individuals took to the
airwaves. By the 1920s, noncommercial stations out-

numbered commercial stations by a ratio of two-to-one. To cope with the explosion of interest, Congress passed the Radio Act of 1927, thereby creating the Federal Radio Commission (FRC), prototype of today's FCC. The purpose of the FRC was to regulate the airwaves "in the public interest, convenience, and necessity."

From 1927 onward, however, the federal government began interpreting its mandate to serve "public interest" in ways utterly inconsistent with that of other branches of government. In the case of libraries, schools, parks, and highways, for example, regulating in the "public interest" has meant preserving those spaces from the presence of business. In the case of the airwaves, this interpretation has been reversed, but not without resistance. As Robert W. McChesney points out, "Between 1928 and 1935, some elements of American society actively opposed the emerging commercial set-up and attempted to have a significant portion of the ether set aside for non-commercial and nonprofit utilization."[1]

"Declaring that the 'public interest, convenience, and necessity' was better served by 'general public ser-

FCC PUBLIC AFFAIRS HEAD ROBERT FISKE STUNNED BY RADIO MUTINY'S NOTORIOUS DJ CONDOM LADY, OUTSIDE FCC HEADQUARTERS, OCTOBER 5, 1998.

GREG RUGGIERO

vice' (i.e. commercial) stations" writes free speech lawyer Robert Perry, "than by 'special interest' and 'propaganda' (i.e., noncommercial) stations, the FRC gave noncommercial stations fewer hours than commercial stations. The FRC also limited broadcast radio licenses to three-month terms, effectively requiring noncommercial stations to expend their limited financial resources fending off license renewal challenges from commercial stations every three months."[2] The FRC's pro-business interpretation of "public interest" served to privatize the airwaves. Noncommercial radio virtually disappeared between 1927 and 1934, shrinking down to barely 2 percent of all radio airtime by 1934.

The passage of the Federal Communications Act of 1934 maintained the seemingly democratic language of the 1927 Act; regulation of the airwaves would be carried out to serve the "public interest, convenience, and necessity," and what was once the FRC then became the FCC. In the 65 years since its inception, the FCC has taken several steps in attempt to fulfill its mandate to serve civil society. To the benefit of commercialism, however, each of these steps has long since been eliminated. At a glance:

1. FAIRNESS DOCTRINE

Genuine democracy requires an informed public that has access to a diverse range of controversial and contrasting views. Thus, in 1949 the FCC adopted the Fairness Doctrine, requiring radio stations to provide reasonable coverage of opposing views on issues of relevance to the community. During the Reagan years, the Fairness Doctrine was eliminated.

2. PUBLIC AFFAIRS PROGRAMMING

Genuine democracy requires media that reflects the cultural diversity and local issues that characterize a community. Thus, the FCC required that 8 percent of AM radio airtime and 6 percent of FM radio airtime be dedicated to public affairs programming that was nonentertainment oriented. As a condition of license renewal, the FCC also required that stations actually study the communities in which they were broadcasting in order to access the needs of the people living there. During the Reagan years, these requirements were all eliminated.

3. MICROPOWER BROADCASTING

Genuine democracy is based on broad public participation, a condition made possible not by political representation, but by direct public access. Beginning in 1948, the FCC permitted public access to the airwaves by issuing "Class D" low power broadcasting licenses to community groups, colleges, and churches. As a result, noncommercial radio flourished for the first time since the 1920s. In 1978, under pressure from an ambitious National Public Radio organization that hoped to consolidate audiences, the FCC enacted a ban on all broadcasting under 100 watts, with no cases of waivers granted to this day.

TELECOMMUNICATIONS REFORM ACT

The general drift toward complete corporate control of the airwaves reached a new extreme with the passage of the Telecommunications Reform Act of 1996. The Act's defining feature is the toleration of a higher limit of media outlets—radio and TV stations—that any one corporation can own. It also eases restrictions preventing these huge media conglomerates from merging into one another—creating enormous, monolithic powers. As microradio scholar Larry Soley observes, "Almost 4,000 or nearly 40 percent, of the nation's roughly 10,300 commercial radio stations have been traded in deals collectively worth $32 billion, with the largest radio station group owners being the most aggressive purchasers. The 10 largest group owners today control 1,134 commercial radio stations, up from 652 prior to passage of the Telecommunications Act of 1996. The Dallas investment firm, Hicks, Muse, Tate & Furst Inc., is the group leader, with over 400 stations, followed by CBS with 175 stations. According to Broadcast Investment Analysts, there are nearly 15 percent fewer radio station owners than there were prior to the passage of the act. Two group owners, CBS and Chancellor Media, today have nearly 53 percent of radio listeners in the top 10 markets, with CBS having 27 percent and Chancellor having 25.2 percent. CBS holds nearly 50 percent of the news/talk listening audience in those markets."[3] And it goes on and on. Corporations get the licenses to broadcast, controlling both access and content. Any lingering obligation to serve "public interest" is completely paved over, and the notion of democracy itself begins to sound vague, abstract. Media corporations are not in business to make democracy possible but, rather, to capture the largest possible audience, whose attention they then sell like scrap metal to advertisers.

This scenario and the policies that protect it provide a clear portrait of the corporate agenda: maintaining the face of a democratic society while pushing laws and policies that decrease the public arena, redefine citizenship in terms of consumerism, and provide unfettered conditions for corporations to evolve with the rights of individuals and the power of nation states. In the resulting free-for-all of corporate mergers, "the public interest" is duly served with a variety of entertainment options, while the spectrum of political and social information reaching public awareness narrows to the point of meaninglessness. The notion of a public discussion pursuing

MEDIA MONOLITH PUPPET, DUPONT CIRCLE,
WASHINGTON, DC, OCTOBER 5, 1998.

any real increase in social welfare, freedom, or self-determination is impossible because there are no longer any
public venues through which to express such thoughts.

"Only 15 percent of AM and FM radio stations are
non-commercial," Soley points out in his superb book
Free Radio: Electronic Civil Disobedience, "and most
are affiliated with NPR, which has effectively kept the
public from participating in program production. In
effect, NPR has functioned as a government-funded bar-
rier to real community broadcasting." Since the U.S.
government demonstrates a commitment to "corporate
rather than public welfare", says Soley, "they cannot be
counted on to protect the public from corporate censorship. If anything, Congress and the FCC have abet-
ted and legalized corporate censorship, and as long as
corporate censorship exists, speech is not free."[4]

"In the current media environment," says Robert
Perry, "speech is merely another commodity to be bought
and sold, valued primarily for it's revenue potential." The

GREG RUGGIERO

resulting blackout on local issues, core political speech, and cultural diversity has not occurred without resistance. Over the past five years, a national movement has mushroomed in opposition to corporate control of communications. This is a movement made up of hundreds of community groups who operate unlicensed clandestine radio stations in much the same spirit that Rosa Parks sat in the front of the bus: to resist and challenge a dehumanizing and unconstitutional system.

NETWORKS OF ALTERNATIVE COMMUNICATION

Everywhere that oppressive restrictions become formally institutionalized by either government or business, there one finds resistance, underground networks, and liberation struggles. Among grassroots groups, there is a growing consensus to use our precious few resources creating *alternatives* to corporate media, rather than attempting to revolutionize the system through head-on confrontation. "Media wealth is too concentrated, too solidified, and too integrated into the corporate-government elite to make social change within the existing system possible," says Project Censored Director, Peter Phillips.

Realizing that corporate power will continue to deny civil society the kinds of information and access that make participatory democracy possible, the Zapatistas have proposed the formation of an "intercontinental network of alternative communication" as a way of sharing movement news, organizing, and celebrating the art and culture of resistance. In his video message to the *Freeing the Media* gathering that took place in New York City two years ago, Subcommandante Marcos said, "We have a choice: we can have a cynical attitude in the face of the media, to say that nothing can be

SUBCOMANDANTE MARCOS, FROM VIDEO MESSAGE ON BUILDING ALTERNATIVE MEDIA NETWORKS, JANUARY 1997. *Picture still from video shot by Kerry Appel*

done ... Or we can simply assume incredulity: we can say that any communication by the media monopolies is a total lie. We can ignore it and go about our lives....But there is a third option that is neither conformity, nor skepticism, nor distrust: that is to construct a different way—to show the world what is really happening....In August 1996, we called for the creation of a network of independent media, a network of information.... We need this network not only as a tool for our social movements but for our lives: this is a project of life, of humanity—humanity which has a right to critical and truthful information." [5]

Alongside the invaluable on-line activism now proliferating via the Internet, the growing network of microradio broadcasters is emerging as an energetic force in building viable, community-oriented alternatives to the corporate agenda. Around the country, hundreds of communities are creating what the Zapatistas call *aguascalientes*,[6]—centers of civil resistance—by operating low-watt radio stations where they can express their cultures, their languages, and their politics with complete freedom—and in complete opposition to corporate control of the public airwaves. "There are literally thousands of Americans who seek to penetrate the Iron Curtain created by the FCC to prevent any significant diversity of voices and opinions from being expressed over the airwaves" says Lou Hiken, attorney for Stephen

GREG RUGGIERO

Dunifer and Free Radio Berkeley. Through email lists, newsletters, gatherings, websites, and cassette tape exchanges, individual underground stations share news, organize events, fine tune strategy, and continually grow a decentralized network that bypasses corporate control of communication.

The network of clandestine microbroadcasters is not a new development. Laurence Soley says it started in Hitler's Germany when the resistance movement there used unlicensed radio as a strategy against the Nazis. In fact, Soley suggests that the presence of clandestine radio corresponds to the degree of repression in a given country. The more people feel a restriction of information and speech, the more that they take to the airwaves. The situation in the U.S. has become so problematic that it has moved beyond the mere *presence* of clandestine stations, toward an increasingly organized and sophisticated national effort. Like the civil rights movement of the 1960s, free radio activists are becoming adept at coordinating multiple tactics—lawsuits against the government, demonstrations, strategy conferences, media campaigns, educational tours, and increasing civil disobedience—all in order to freely communicate.

MICROBROADCASTERS IN THE STREETS

On October 4 & 5, 1998, for example, hundreds of activists gathered in Washington, DC for a national microradio conference and protest of federal communications policies and the corporate forces that shape it. Over the weekend, microradio activists sent a team of lobbyists to meet with representatives on Capitol Hill, launched a new DC station (Radio Libre), staged a panel at the Freedom Forum that was broadcast to 86 countries, and conducted dozens of interviews with the mainstream press, resulting in coverage in the *Washington Post*, NPR, MSNBC, and many others. The weekend culminated with a massive march and puppet parade from Dupont Circle to FCC headquarters, and then on to the headquarters of the National Association of Broadcasters (NAB)—the pro-industry group that most intensely pressures the FCC to stamp out microbroadcasting. DC cops on motorcycles blocked swarmed around protesters as they marched through the streets blocking intersections and stopping traffic. Bread and Puppet Theater-esque puppets showed FCC Chairman "Kennardio" in the likeness of Pinnochio being controlled by a bigger puppet, a TV-headed monster (the NAB), which, in turn, was being puppeteered by an even larger, more hideous looking beast: the corporate media monolith. The march came to a head when microbroadcasters overpowered NAB agents (attempting to keep marchers off headquarters' property), hauled the NAB flag down from the top of a high pole, and rose up in its place a pirate radio flag. The action filled the air with cheers of joy, and resulted in two arrests.

The entire two-day program was organized by volunteers with next to no resources. Full housing and deliciously prepared food were provided to most conference goers for a one-time registration fee, five bucks in most cases. The weekend in DC is just a small example of the degree of dedication, commitment, and planning now being waged by activists dead set on reclaiming the airwaves for democratic purposes.

MICRORADIO IN THE COURTROOM: THE CASE OF FREE RADIO BERKELEY

Until now, the FCC has done everything possible to avoid having the constitutionality of its regulations for-

COPS ARREST TWO ACTIVISTS OUTSIDE NAB
HEADQUARTERS, WASHINGTON, DC, OCTOBER 5, 1998.

mally challenged. For more than two years, the micropower radio movement was watching the case of Stephen Dunifer and Free Radio Berkeley, hoping that Judge Claudia Wilken would consider the FCC's ban unconstitutional and rule in favor of microbroadcasting. But on Tuesday, June 16, 1998, shock waves rippled through the micropower radio movement as a short message from Stephen Dunifer coursed through e-mail networks across the Internet. Dunifer's message read: "We just received notification that Federal Judge Claudia Wilken has granted the FCC motion for summary judgement for a permanent injunction against myself and all others acting in concert with me." Two days later Dunifer's station, Free Radio Berkeley, was off the air.

Free Radio Berkeley first took to the airwaves in the spring of 1993. In November 1993, the FCC busted the station, fining Dunifer $20,000 for broadcasting without a license. In the legal battle that ensued, the FCC sought a court injunction against Dunifer, an injunction which Judge Claudia Wilken denied on January 30, 1995 for two reasons: first, because Dunifer had raised significant constitutional challenges; and, second, because the FCC was unable to prove that any harm would result if Free Radio Berkeley continued to broadcast.

Judge Wilken did not shut down Dunifer, because his constitutional challenges were overruled. In fact, throughout Judge Wilken's 20-page decision, she manages to completely *avoid* answering the constitutional questions that Dunifer raises as his defense. Instead, Judge Wilken bases her ruling against him on a technical Catch-22: that Dunifer never applied for a license. "This ruling is not based on the merits of Mr. Dunifer's criticism of the FCC's refusal to license microbroadcasters... Mr. Dunifer does not have standing as required by Article III of the United States Constitution to challenge the Class D regulations as they have been applied to him; because he has never applied for a license."[7]

Dunifer's attorneys are contesting Judge Wilken's decision. On Monday, June 29, they filed a Motion to Alter Judgement and requested a hearing for August 7. Their motion argues that Wilken is in error, and the logic of applying for a license and a waiver as prerequisites to challenging the constitutionality of the FCC's microradio ban is like demanding that Rosa Parks ask for a waiver to sit on the front of the bus. "The obstacle course that the F.C.C. has established for licensing full-power commercial broadcasters is so daunting and overwhelming," writes Lou Hiken, "that no microstation could ever pass muster in that context. It is as if the government demanded that mothers taking splinters out of their childrens' fingers comply with the regulatory requirements for an institution engaging in heart surgery."[8]

GREG RUGGIERO

As stated in Dunifer's June 29, 1998 Motion to Alter Judgment, Judge Wilken's decision means that "all those who have awaited the opportunity to have a federal court resolve on the merits the constitutional issues surrounding access to the airwaves have been told that they must refrain from broadcasting for the months and years that it will take them to apply to the FCC for waivers and to receive the certain denials that will be issued. That is a cruel hoax upon thousands of Americans who want nothing more than the right to speak over their own airwaves..."[9]

Dunifer was not granted a hearing on August 7, 1998. Judge Wilken said that she did not require oral presentations in order to determine if she would amend her judgement. Whether or not she does, public unrest over the ban on microradio has and will continue to mount until some form of community access to the airwaves has been realized. Dunifer's civil disobedience, like that of Rosa Parks, has ignited a mass movement. As a result of his activism, communities all over America are claiming a seat in the front of the airwaves, challenging the injustice of the FCC's licensing scheme despite the very real threat of raid, bust, and seizure of property. During a 10 month period in 1998 alone, FCC Chairman Kennard claims to have shut down more than 250 stations, many with the help of armed Federal Marshalls.[10]

STEAL THIS RADIO 88.7FM, NYC

With the presence of several underground stations and the support of activist groups like the New York Free Media Alliance, Paper Tiger Television, FAIR and the Center for Constitutional Rights, New York City has become a hot spot for free media organizing. At the center of the local micro resistance is Steal This Radio

STEAL THIS RADIO DEMONSTRATION AND
PRESS CONFERENCE, APRIL 15, 1998.

(STR), a 20-watt station that has been broadcasting at
88.7 fm for three years on the Lower East Side.

In March 1998, Steal This Radio was visited by
Judah Mansbach, a notorious FCC agent responsible for
hunting down scores of pirate stations. Following Mansbach's visit, STR decided to temporarily go off the air
until the station was able to strike first against the FCC
with a full-scale legal/media assault. That action
began on April 15, 1998, when STR held a demonstration and press conference at the site where George
Washington took oath as first President of the United
States (directly across from the New York Stock
Exchange). That afternoon, Steal This Radio's lawyers
formally initiated the lawsuit by submitting papers in
Federal court.

Steal This Radio's case is called *Free Speech vs. the
FCC* and is represented by two brilliant lawyers, Robert
Perry and Barbara Olshansky from The Center For Constitutional Rights. Their legal offensive establishes that
the airwaves are a public forum and, as such, are a venue

GREG RUGGIERO

where free speech should be protected by the Constitution. The FCC's condition that broadcasters take to the airwaves at 100 watts or more is one that involves an investment of hundreds of thousands of dollars—resources no community group has at its disposal. (Free speech lawyer Alan Korn compares the situation to being in a public park but only being permitted to exercise free speech if you own a 24-karat gold box to stand on.) STR's case also argues that the FCC's procedure for raiding stations and seizing equipment is illegal, even under the FCC's own statute, the Communications Act of 1934. "In other words," says Perry, "it's the FCC that is breaking the law."

Despite the government's aggressive campaign against low power broadcasting, Olshansky and Perry are optimistic. Unlike Dunifer's *defensive* case against the FCC, STR's case is *offensive*; and, also unlike Dunifer's case, which challenged the FCC 's regulations *as applied to him in his unique set of circumstances*, Steal This Radio's challenge attacks the FCC's licensing scheme as a whole, asserting that it is unconstitutional on its face, not just as applied to STR. For these reasons, Steal This Radio's case has the potential to bring down the FCC's pro-corporate licensing scheme.

Along the way, Steal This Radio has already scored one small victory. In an 8 page decision issued on February 1, 1999, by U.S. District Judge Michael Mukasey, the FCC's motion against STR plaintiffs filing their lawsuit under fictious names was *denied*. Plaintiffs DJ Thomas Paine, DJ Carlos Rising, DJ Sharin, DJ E.S.E., etc, on behalf of Steal This Radio, are thus protected to pursue their lawsuit against the FCC using assumed names. In Judge Mukasey's own words, "To deny them permission to proceed by pseudonym would either expose plaintiffs to further penalties and prosecution or, more likely than not, discourage them from pursuing their constitutional challenge."[11]

On Tuesday March 16, 1999 Judge Mukasey ruled against Steal This Radio's challenge of the FCC, ruling that the airwaves are a "non-public forum." "Given plaintiffs' three-year-long, nearly continuous violations of the licensing requirement, there is every indication that plaintiffs will continue to violate this provision in the future unless restrained by judicial order. Accordingly, the government's request for a preliminary injunction is granted,"[12] reads Mukasey's decision.

"It's a sad day for freedom of speech on the airwaves" said Robert Perry upon learning of the decision. According to Perry, Judge Mukasey "misstated the facts of the case, rejected and then misapplied our public forum analysis."

Robert Perry and Barbara Olshansky are seeking a stay against the injunction and are filing an appeal in 2nd circuit federal court. "This is just the first round" says Perry, "this case has a shot at making it all the way to the Supreme Court."

PETITIONS FOR RULEMAKING

Outside the courtroom, microbroadcasters have also been using channels opened by the FCC themselves to alter regulation. Several petitions seeking to legalize microradio have been recognized by the FCC. Two of these petitions are meaningless tokens: RM-9208 proposes low power license of 1 watt or less (which basically means shouting distance), and RM-9246 proposes "Event Broadcast Stations" to provide temporary stations access to the airwaves. The third petition, RM-9242, is more sophisticated. Proposed by J. Rodger

Skinner, it proposes the creation of three new classes of low power stations: one of up to 50 watts, one 50 watts to 3 kilowatts, and a third for the creation of temporary stations. In order to insure that these stations are a true organ of community, the petition proposes that license holders live within a 50-mile radius of the station and that no licensee would be permitted to own more than 3 stations nationwide. In this petition, micropower stations are called "secondary service stations" and are designated "to those types of of broadcasters who do not wish to conform to a more structured and/ or regulated form of broadcasting." Good as this may sound, this petition too is seriously flawed. Skinner proposes this license as being deferential to commercial interests,"[T]he licensee must vacate the channel," writes Skinner, "if a full-power station becomes short spaced . . . due to an antenna site move or power increase, or application by a...primary service applicant." Skinner's idea here is not to create sovereign community stations but, rather, to provide a temporary slot for folks who are planning to "upgrade" to a "full-power" station.

Even though these are the only three petitions that the FCC have formally presented for public comment, new regulations are by no means constrained by these three petitions alone. The National Lawyers Guild Committee for Democratic Communications (CDC) has submitted a proposal that most accurately expresses the micro radio movement's noncommercial, self-determined, public interest core. The CDC are the in-for-the-long-haul, free media activist lawyers who've been fighting for microbroadcasters since 1989. Their mission is to focus "on the rights of all peoples to have a worldwide system of media and communications based upon the principle of cultural and informational self-determination." As an alternative to the three petitions which the FCC presented for public commentary, the CDC proposed, and won wide support for, new regulation that would permit:

1. Noncommercial service
2. Only one station per owner
3. Local ownership, no absentee owners
4. That stations shall be locally programmed. However, recorded materials (such as music, poetry, documentaries, features, etc.) may be used. Sharing of program materials and resources among micro and community stations is strongly encouraged.
5. That owners be individuals, unincorporated associations, or nonprofit organizations. For-profit corporations, partnerships, joint ventures, or other organizations may not be owners.
6. That stations may be established on any unused frequency within the fm broadcast band down to 87.5. Second adjacent channel would be the closest spacing allowed.
7. That maximum power shall be 100 watts. In the event of interference due to power level, a station shall have the option to reduce power to remedy the situation or be shut down.
8. That a microstation shall fill out a simple registration form, and send one copy with an appropriate registration fee to the FCC and a second copy to the voluntary body set up by the micropower broadcast community to oversee the micropower stations.
9. That equipment shall meet a basic technical criteria in respect to stability, filtering, modulation control, etc.
10. That registration shall be valid for four years.
11. That there shall be no specific public service requirements imposed by the FCC.
12. That problems, whether technical or otherwise,

shall be first referred to the local or regional voluntary micropower organization for technical assistance or voluntary mediation. The FCC shall be the forum of last resort.

13. That when television broadcast stations go digital, leaving Channel 6 free, it shall be allocated as an extension to the bottom of the fm band strictly for low-power community fm service. Radio receivers manufactured or entering the country after that allocation must meet this band extension.

14. That microbroadcasting of special events (demonstrations, protests, rallies, festivals, concerts, etc.) do not need to be registered but are encouraged to meet all technical specifications.

THE FCC'S NEW PROPOSAL

Intense and sustained pressure from microbroadcasters' civil disobedience strategies, lawsuits, and media campaigns have clearly impacted the government. Confirmation of this came two weeks after the October 98 protests, when FCC head William Kennard stood before the sworn enemies of microbroadcasting, the National Association of Broadcasters (NAB), and signalled his intention to soon lift the microradio ban.[13] Three months later, Kennard's intention materialized. On January 28, 1999, at a public meeting that was broadcast live over the Internet[14] the FCC released a Notice of Proposed Rulemaking (NPRM) to legalize a new set of microradio licenses.[15]

The FCC's proposal to legalize microradio is an exciting development, and Chairman Kennard deserves some credit for what looks like responsiveness to the grassroots and an openly defiant posture against the broadcasting industry. Despite this, features in the FCC's proposal disfavor a genuinely civic, community oriented vision of microradio licensing. In the words of Phil Tymon:

> The FCC has gone a good part of the way in envisioning a new type of radio service, an entirely new model. But we urge the FCC to go even further. It appears that a variety of goals and motivations underlie the FCC's current proposal. Some of those goals appear contradictory to us. As such, there is no coherent and cohesive theory that consistently underlies the FCC's proposal. We fear that the contradictions may eventually unravel the entire fabric of this new service and vitiate its dynamic ability to bring fresh, new, vibrant voices to American communities. Without a clear, consistent vision of what this new service should be, we believe there is a great risk that ten years down the road the small loopholes will have grown to freeways, and the same forces that have so enervated the creative spirit of current radio will dominate in LPFM.[16]

One of the major contradictions of the NPRM is it's proposal that small neighborhood stations of 100 watts or less assume a secondary, deferential status to new 1000 watt stations. In other words, if a community group in Harlem has a successful 40 watt station up and running and a business group comes along with a 1000 watt license, the little community group—perhaps several of them in the area—will all have to forfeit their licenses in order to make room for the one commercial 1000 watt station.

Furthermore, the FCC's NPRM proposes that microradio pioneers who sparked and fueled the movement with civil disobedience not be permitted to receive licenses when micro is legalized. The FCC have argued that such people, by virtue of their disobedience, establish that they will be "unreliable" license holders. By this logic, the FCC might have agreed that runaway slaves not be granted full freedom after the Emancipation Proclamation because they would make "unreliable" citizens. It's precisely these people who take the risks and push the envelope of power far enough to make change a real possibility. Not granting Mbanna Kantako or Stephen Dunifer a license would be like not letting Rosa Parks sit in the front of the bus. "There are times to break free of the mind numbing procedures and forms of language of bureaucracy. This is one of them," says Phil Tymon. "The FCC must admit that this proceeding is occurring not out of the goodness of the government's heart, but solely because the unlicensed microbroadcasters have refused to back down, have refused to be silenced.The pioneers of microradio must be given the opportunity to be LPFM broadcasters. Any other result would be immoral."[17]

Of course there are obstacles. The biggest threat to micro is the National Association of Broadcasters—one of America's most powerful lobbies— which is rabid with opposition to any form of microradio.[18] In a meeting with the NAB on February 11, 1999, Representative Billy Tauzin (R-Louisiana), called the NPRM "ill advised" and said the FCC "is an agency out of control that demands congressional action to straighten it out."[19] Tauzin, who is chair of the House Commerce Committee's communications subcommittee, was expressing the broadcasting industry's fear of competition. It's no secret that the NAB's war against micro is rooted in the possibility of listeners defecting from the monoculture of corporate stations to ad-free neighborhood stations that directly express the languages, news, tastes and culture of the communities in which they live. The NAB claim that microstations will create interference, an argument that even Chairman Kennard calls a "smokescreen" for the industry's real concern: eliminating the competition created by more democracy.

The second threat to the community application of microradio comes from groups who seek to end the ban, but which see microradio as a profit making device for private owners. Among the most visible groups advocating the pro-commercial model is The Media Access Project, a Washington D.C. based group with close ties to the FCC. MAP's advocacy work is particularly problematic because it tucks private sector advocacy under a "public interest" banner. MAP seems to forget that each cubic millimeter of public space that goes over to private control— be it a library, a park, a school, or an unused piece of radio spectrum—is a space where civic access is denied and our powers of citizenship are lost. The purpose of legalizing non-commercial microradio is to grant communities the power to make their own media and tell their own stories. The struggle for non-commercial microradio is thus a struggle for citizenship and free speech in the electronic age. Anything less is not in the "public interest."

RESPONSE TO THE FCC'S PROPOSAL

On the side of the free radio movement, the National Lawyers Guild Committee of Democratic Communications' Phil Tymon is leading the way with analysis and comments on the government's proposal. His impressive first draft of CDC's comments went out over microradio email lists on March 20, 1999:

The promise of a new LPFM service is that of:
- Local programming designed for local communities,
- Diverse and alternative voices and viewpoints,
- Service to currently unserved communities.

We propose that all decisions related to LPFM be measured by two guiding principles:

1. Encourage use of LPFM by those who have an urgent desire to communicate above all else—whether that be communication of information, ideas, art, or culture. Discourage those who wish to use LPFM as a means of making money.

2. Encourage maximum diversity of voices and viewpoints.

Wherever a decision needs to be made regarding implementation of LPFM these two principles should be applied.

Wherever a decision needs to be made regarding implementation of LPFM these two principles should be applied.

We Support a Complete Amnesty for Microradio Pioneers

We Support Allocation of New Spectrum for LPFM

We support the establishment of a 100 Watt LPFM service. We believe the service should have the following features:

1. Non-commercial (including no "underwriting" announcements)

2. License/Registration Non-Transferable

3. Primary status, modified to allow more liberal receipt of interference

4. Local programming requirements

5. Ownership requirements:

a. One to an owner (local and national)

   b. Local residency requirement

   c. No ownership by those with full-power radio license (local and national)

   d. No ownership by those with full- or low- power TV license (local and national)

   e. No ownership by those with ownership interest in other mass media such as telephone company, cable TV company, satellite broadcaster, daily newspaper, etc.

We urge the Commission NOT to adopt a 1,000 watt LPFM service, with the exception of very rural areas.

We urge an application, regulatory, and renewal system based largely in voluntary local self-regulation.[20]

Many grassroots groups are organizing around the proposal in addition to the CDC. Citizens' Media Corps, a Massachusetts based group that formed in the wake of the FCC's seizure of Free Radio Allston, is mobilizing a letter-writing campaigns to pressure the FCC. Stephen Provizer, founder of Citizens' Media Corps, states: "If they prioritize commercial licensing, it's not much of a victory, if they make it more community friendly, it will be a testament, I believe, to the energy and persistence of those who have an unshakable belief in the importance of citizen access to media." [21]

Also mobilizing around the legalization process is the Microradio Empowerment Coalition, a newly formed group whose purpose is to win non-commercial legalization of microradio. "The radio spectrum is already dominated by commercial forces" says Sara Zia Ebrahimi, one of the Coalition's steering committee members. "From the way the NAB is reacting, you'd think we were calling for a complete redistribution of spectrum or asking that some of the bigger stations to scale down to make room for a more new stations. Great ideas, but we're not pushing that far. What we're talking about is accessing the last few remaining slivers of available spectrum and using them for democratic purposes—for free speech by non-commercial community groups." To win non-commercial legalization, the Microradio Empowerment Coalition is bringing together a diverse group of organizations like Fairness and Accuracy in Reporting, Libraries for the Future, Media Education Foundation, CDC, the Center For Constitutional Rights among many others, to write letters to the FCC and to help with public education. "With so much of our media dominated by commercialism," said Ebrahimi, "it would be offensive to fill the remaining cracks in the radio spectrum with the advertising and commercials that "microbusiness" stations will dump on local audiences."

Sister groups like the Prometheus Radio Project, another newly formed microradio advocacy group, recently completed a six week tour of the east coast to raise awareness on the issues. Free public workshops were held at community centers and info shops. When the group came to New York City on February 27, 1999, approximately 150 people came out to learn about the issues, how to file comments with the FCC, where to get equipment, and how to start stations of their own—with or without a license from the FCC. "If the new rules are reasonable, the Prometheus Radio Project will encourage people to abide by them, and we'll be working hard to assist the many former radio "pirates" and community groups that need access to the airwaves in their applications for licenses. There's nothing we'd like to see more than an orderly transition to a new way of doing things, by all the parties in this struggle," said Pete tri Dish, co-founder of the Prometheus Radio Project and former member of Philadelphia's Radio Mutiny. Prometheus, like many grassroots groups springing up around the country, will use the opportunity of the NPRM to heighten public desire for it's own system of communication.

While the NPRM proposes to legalize microradio, it is far from clear what kind of service, if any, may finally be realized. Whether the new licenses will favor commercial or non commercial applicants, whether large 1000 watt licenses will be favored over issuing several 100 watt licenses, whether stations that have been shut down by the FCC will be permitted to apply, and whether or not it's easy to apply for a license are all issues that are still very much up for grabs, and media and democracy activists still have every opportunity to influence any final outcome. This is one of those relatively rare times when a government agency creates an opening for the public to counter corporate power and overcome it. And there is every chance that we will.

MICROBROADCASTING AND DEMOCRACY

"Democracy functions insofar as individuals can participate meaningfully in the public arena," writes Chomsky, "while running their own affairs, individually and collectively, without illegitimate interference by concentrations of power." With this definition in mind, it's disturbingly clear that we live in a dysfunctional democracy at best, where public arenas and the means

GREG RUGGIERO

to participate in them are as segregated as Rosa Parks' bus. Corporate powers control communications and decision making, while civil society is marginalized, community speech banned, and our active powers of citizenship are perversely redefined to mean our passive choice as shoppers.

Establishment media have become the *Niña*, *Pinta*, and *Santa Maria* of commercialism, forcing upon the shores of our consciousness a permanent invasion of unwanted, coercive, and alienating messages. They deliver the unspoken ideology that representation is reality, ownership is identity, and that to consume is to connect. As a counter-offensive to this degrading assault on our everyday lives, the most effective use of our resources may not be to engage the commercial media system head-on but, rather, to concentrate on building sustainable new venues and alternative networks. For those with computers the Internet provides immediate possibilities for entering such a network, possibilities being realized through the efforts of groups like Tao Communications in Toronto, and others elsewhere. For those without access, for those who cannot read, for those with few resources, for those who struggle, micropower radio is a powerful weapon, a source, an invitation, a resistance, a connection...

Like Rosa Parks, we are not willing to wait for court cases or petition results to sit in the front of the airwaves. As enormous corporations merge and rival nation states for real global power, regaining control of communications at the local level represents a genuine revolution, a grassroots insurgency to advance our basic human freedoms and to place public access to communications at the heart of our everyday lives. Like the Zapatistas, we will continue to organize, continue to agitate, continue to seek one another out at meetings, over the airwaves, and in the streets until we have won the freedom and the resources to realize genuine democracy, a necessary victory, but not an end, in the struggle to build a better world.

NOTES

* "(Low) Power to the People" is the title of an article by Geov Parrish that appeared in *Mother Jones*, March 9, 1999.

1. Robert W. McChesney, *Telecommunications, Mass Media, & Democracy: The Battle for the Control of U.S. Broadcasting, 1928-1935* (Oxford University Press, 1993): 3f. An invaluable book for anyone interested in understanding the origins of U.S. radio policy, how commercial forces gained

GREG RUGGIERO

control of the airwaves, and how the public organized and resisted.

2. Robert Perry and Barbara Olshansky, quoted from "The First Amended Complaint, *Free Speech vs. the FCC*, May 12, 1998." Full text see: http://artcon.rutgers.edu/papertiger/nyfma. Much of the info here on U.S. communications history was gleaned by studying their papers.

3. Quoted from Larry Soley's July 2, 1998 affidavit in the *Free Speech vs. the FCC* lawsuit.

4. Lawrence Soley, *Free Radio: Electronic Civil Disobedience* (Westview Press, 1999): p46.

5. The Zapatistas' original proposal said "Let's make a network of communication among all our struggles and resistances. An intercontinental network of alternative communication against neoliberalism...(and) for humanity. This intercontinental network of alternative communication will search to weave the channels so that words may travel all the roads that resist...(it) will be the medium by which distinct resistances communicate with one another. This intercontinental network of alternative communication is not an organizing structure, nor has a central head or decision maker, nor does it have a central command or hierarchies. We are the network, all of us who speak and listen."

    Complete text of the Zapatista proposals are published in the Open Media Pamphlet, *Zapatista Encuentro* available from Seven Stories Press (800. 596. 7437). Complete footage of Subcommandante's video message is available from Paper Tiger TV (212. 940. 2045).

6. *Aguascalientes* literally means "hot water." In the Zapatista democracy struggle, *Aguascalientes* refers to the civilian cultural resistance centers that serve surrounding communities by providing a space for political meetings, cultural events, dialogue and "*encuentros*" with civil society, as well as being places that contain schools, women's cooperatives, and health clinics.

    The first *Aguascalientes* was destroyed by federal troops after they occupied the township of Guadelupe Tepeyac on February 5, 1995. In 1994 it was the site of the Democratic National Convention where 6,000 people from Mexico and all over the world gathered to meet with the Zapatistas and dialogue about the possibility of building an international movement of resistance "for humanity and against neoliberalism."

    Here in the U.S., microradio stations serve many of the same functions as the Zapatistas' civil resistance centers—providing space for political discussion, cultural events, organizing, dialogue, and exchange. In this light, microradio stations are our *Aguascalientes* of the airwaves.

7. Quoted from Judge Claudia Wilken's June 16, 1998 decision. For the complete text see: http://www.368Hayes.com/wilkenrules.html.

8 . Lou Hiken, excerpted from his June 29, 1998 Motion for Judge Clau-

dia Wilken to Alter Judgment in her decision against Stephen Dunifer. Complete text of his motion is available at: http://www.368Hayes.com/microradio.mtn_to_alter.htm>

9. Ibid

10. Statistic taken from FCC Chairman Kennard's October 16, 1998 speech to the National Association of Broadcasters. For complete text of his speech see: www.fcc.gov/commissioners/kennard/speeches

11. Quoted from U.S. District Judge Michael B. Mukasey's Opinion and Order filed in on February 1, 1999 in reference to the *Free Speech vs. the FCC*. See the New York Free Media Alliance web page for the complete text: http://artcon.rutgers.edu/papertiger/nyfma/

12. Quoted from Judge Mukasey's March 16, 1999 decision against Steal This Radio. See the New York Free Media Alliance web page for the complete text: http://artcon.rutgers.edu/papertiger/nyfma/

13. For complete text of this historic speech see: www.fcc.gov/commissioners/kennard/speeches

14. For a complete audio file of the January 28, 1999 public meeting see: http://www.fcc.gov/realaudio

15. Complete text of the FCC's Notice of Proposed Rulemaking on microradio is available at: http://www.fcc.gov/Bureaus/Mass_Media/Notices/1999/fcc99006.txt

16. Phil Tymon, from first draft Comments of the National Lawyers Guild Committee On Democratic Communications, posted over microradio@tao.ca email list by Lynn Gerry on March 19, 1999. See CDC's web site for the text of CDC's complete and final comments on the NPRM (http://www.nlgcdc.org/).

17. Ibid

18. For more information on the National Association of Broadcasters, check out http://www.radio4all.org/nab/index.html which has, among other things a link to a 400 page study on the NAB's influence in Washington done by Common Cause. Also see the NAB's declaration of war at http://www.radio4all.org/news/nabwar.html

19. Ibid, Phil Tymon.

20. Quoted from a Reuters news wire by Aaron Pressman, "Top Legislator Blasts FCC Microradio Proposal," February 12, 1999.

21. Quoted from Seeta Peña Gangadharan's excellent article, "Microradio: The Noise You Can't Ignore" distributed on-line by Alternet 77 Federal Street, San Francisco, CA 94107. Email: khayes@igc.org

Appendix A

THE FIGHT FOR MICRORADIO
ENTERS THE HOME STRETCH:
PARADISE OR PARADISE LOST?

PETER FRANCK

For the last ten years the National Lawyers Guild's Committee on Democratic Communications (CDC) has
worked to defend the rights of microradio broadcasters.
Dubbed by their enemies as "pirate radio," microbroadcasters have challenged the government's ban on
affordable, low power, community based radio. They
have challenged it by going on the air in a campaign of
civil disobedience, and supported by movement lawyers
like CDC and the Center for Constitutional Rights, they
have challenged it in court.

Bowing to the power of this movement, the Federal
Communications Commission (FCC) has announced
that it is considering legalizing low power FM. This
move is led by the FCC's chairman William Kennard. It
is opposed by the National Association of Broadcasters
and their friends in Congress.

We have come much further than we would have
dared to hope ten, or even five years ago. But as the microradio movement seems headed for victory it could equally
well be headed for defeat at the hands of the FCC.
Whether we are about to win the addition of a new democratic grassroots community radio to the FM band, or
whether the initiative will be crushed by the overwhelming pressure from the corporate sector will be
decided over the course of 1999. The outcome is very
much up for grabs. We very well may look back on the
period of 1989-1998 as the golden age of microradio—the

period of civil disobedience, movement building, and freedom—albeit clandestine. On January 28, 1999, the FCC after much build up and anticipation, issued a document called a NPRM or Notice of Proposed Rulemaking, in which they proposed to legalize low power FM radio.

SOME BACKGROUND

By releasing a NPRM on microradio, the FCC triggered the final stage of a ten-year battle to create low power, locally oriented community radio. As New Signals Press said in their press release on the subject: "this will be the first new, free, over the air radio broadcasting service the FCC has proposed to create in decades." Given the crowding of the spectrum, it may also be the last.

In the context of this proceeding, a major contest for this space is developing. It is important to understand that within the "microradio movement" there are several distinct groups. The pioneers of microradio are those who have committed the civil disobedience which has brought us to this point, essentially in the tradition of Ghandi and Martin Luther King, by insisting on exercising their constitutional rights (ie, broadcasting without a license despite the federal prohibition). They have forced the FCC to recognize the fact that the government ban on low power radio is both unenforceable, and vulnerable to constitutional attack in the courts. These grassroots groups want to use microradio stations to give voice and empowerment to communities of all kinds, to workers, the poor, immigrants, women, minorities, students, and the list goes on.

On the other hand there is a strong group of would-be broadcast radio entrepreneurs who see this service as a lower tier of the commercial radio industry. They want the FCC to authorize commercial, advertising -based low

GREG RUGGIERO

power stations, and to auction the spectrum space off to the highest bidders. While no one would deny them the right to find a new way to make a living, the fact remains that the paucity of diversity of views and culture available on the airwaves today is a direct result of the pressures that arise from the fact that it is paid for by advertising. More but smaller commercial stations aren't going to change this.

The announcement of the NPRM was preceded by a major public relations campaign mounted by the FCC and its supporters pushing for public support for a new low power radio service as an answer to the consolidation of media (and in particular radio) ownership in the wake of the 1996 rewriting of the telecommunications law of the United States. However, many in the microradio movement are very disappointed with the FCC's proposal. The NPRM tentatively outlines the issues the FCC faces and puts out for public comment the ways that the FCC proposes to handle such issues. Unfortunately, the FCC's proposals are more oriented toward opening the doors to a new group of media entrepreneurs than to opening the doors for non-commercial community groups. Our task is to educate the public and civic groups to the need to ensure that this new service is democratic: non-profit, non-commercial and local. The FCC's initial proposal is weak from our point of view because:

1. It proposes 1000-watt commercially oriented stations. These will take up too much precious spectrum space in the already crowded airwaves of the urban areas. Several small stations can serve many neighborhoods much more directly than can one large station.

2. The FCC proposes to give secondary status to the lower power, more truly community oriented stations (10-100 watts). This means that any thousand watt sta-

tion or any full power station could force the smaller station off the air any time the bigger station wants to shift frequency or increase power. Secondary status guarantees a lack of permanence and a lack of stability.

3. The commission proposes to use lotteries if there are more applications for low power stations in a particular community than there is room for, which is a virtual certainty in all major cities. Lotteries would put an individual who wants to "hear himself talk" or wants to play nothing but his favorite music on an equal footing with a non-profit community group which wants to address concerns of, for example, the farm workers in a particular community. In the context of changes the FCC proposes in how it gives out full power non-commercial licenses, it is considering using a point system to evaluate competing applications. This may be a much better way to go for micro stations, as well.

4. Most important, the commission seems to plan to restrict non-commercial micro stations to the limited air space that can be found in the lower, non-commercial portion of the FM band, leaving the rest of the space to commercial micro stations. This will result in four times as many commercial low power stations as to non-commercial ones. To make matters much worse, the law requires licenses for commercial stations to be auctioned to the highest bidders. This means that four-fifths of these new stations will go to the wealthy organizations which can outbid other groups.

5. The FCC proposes to allow a single organization to own and control up to five low power stations. If what we are after is democratizing the airwaves and giving communities a voice, there is no need at all to let one organization own and control stations in five different communities.

6. The current proposal contains no provisions requir-

GREG RUGGIERO

ing local origination of programming. This would allow wealthy organization to buy up a license and program it by satellite with no involvement from the local community. There is much too much of that on the FM band already!

WHAT IS TO BE DONE?

The CDC has helped to form the Microradio Empowerment Coalition (MEC) to mount a public campaign for truly democratic, locally based microradio service. The purpose of the Coalition is to forge together public interest organizations to support non-commercial legalization of microradio.

The issuance of the NPRM opened a period of formal Public Comment. This is the formal procedure by which the FCC seeks and accepts comment from the public, including concerned civic organizations and coalitions on their proposal. After the public comment period closes on June 1, there will be a thirty-day period for reply comments (to be filed by July 1). After that the Commission staff will summarize all the comments filed, the five Commissioners will decide on the kind of low power FM to authorize. Rules will be drafted and could be issued late in 1999, or early in the year 2000. After the formal comment period closes, we will continue to lobby the FCC on the kind of rules which we feel should be adopted, and continue to engage in public advocacy for democractic, public access to the airwaves.

A campaign of public education and coalition building of community groups is urgently needed. We need to quickly reach, engage, educate, and mobilize organizations such as labor unions, advocacy groups, churches, national consumer groups, community organizations, law students, and others.

In spite of opposition from the National Association of Broadcasters and some rumblings in Congress, recent events, such as a favorable editorial in the industry trade journal *Radio World*, seem to make it clear that there will be some form of low power radio enacted by the FCC. The challenge to community and democracy oriented organizations and individuals is to clearly and forcefully express to the FCC that there is no point in doing this if it is simply going to create a group of want-to-be Chancellor Media and NBC radios.

The Microradio Empowerment Coalition (MEC) has been formed to bring together the forces for a democratic and meaningful new kind of community based radio stations in the FM band: to create and bring to the airwaves new voices, new ideas, new music, and new culture. To join the coalition or for more information about it go to http:www.nlgcdc.org or email to <mec@tao.ca>.

Appendix B

WHAT YOU CAN DO

Write letters to the FCC and your Congressional representatives—many of whom are among the biggest lap
dogs for corporate control of our public resources, and
the biggest obstacles for legalizing microradio. Demand
legalization and prioritizing of non-commercial, low
power, community-based FM radio. Take the easy route!
Use the sample letter below, or if you've got a bit more
time, draft one of your own).

• Write to advocacy groups like The Media Access Project and ask them to reconsider their support for pro-
business, commercial legalization of microradio.
Remind them that the airwaves are already dominated
by commercial interests and that the last remaining slivers of available spectrum would best serve the public
interest if we consider them the way we consider public libraries, schools, or parks: OFF LIMITS to commercialism. Media Access Project: 1707 L Street, NW,
Washington, DC 20036 (202) 232-4300

• Contact the Microradio Empowerment Coalition
whose purpose is to win non-*commercial* legalization of
microradio. Among the Coalition's members are
National Lawyers Guild Committee on Democratic
Communications, Fairness and Accuracy in Reporting,
Media Alliance, Media Education Foundation, Libraries
for The Future, Project Censored, Paper Tiger Television,
New York Free Media Alliance, and many others. Prin-

ciples and documents can be found at many websites including: http://www.nlgcdc.org.

SAMPLE LETTER TO THE FCC:

Federal Communications Commission
Attn: NPRM # FCC 99-6
445 12 Street, S.W. Washington, D.C. 20554
(202) 418-0260
Email: wkennard@fcc.gov
sness@fcc.gov
hfurchtg@fcc.gov
mpowell@fcc.gov
gtristan@fcc.gov
fccinfo@fcc.gov

Re: NPRM # FCC 99-6, MM Docket # 99-25 & #95-25:

I urge you to adopt rules for licensing Low Power FM radio that prioritize the needs of under-served and under-financed communities. Your office has the power and the mandate to ensure that ordinary people can claim a piece of the pie that big corporations have dominated and controlled for years. I am confident you agree that broad citizen access to information and culture is at the heart of a democratic society.

To support this vision, I urge you to legalize micro-radio with the following concerns in mind:

1. This should be a completely non-commercial service. The current radio spectrum is dominated by commercial media. LPFM licenses should go to non-commercial community groups who want to use radio to communicate to the constituents and their neighbors, not to make a profit.It should always be free of the muting

influence that pleasing advertisers Ialways carries with it.

2. Microradio licenses should be held locally, be non-transferable, affordable to all communities, easy to apply for and limited to one per license holder; they should NOT be businesses.

3. Power levels should be up to 100 watts in urban areas and up to 250 watts in rural areas.

4. No secondary status should be allowed, that is, micro-stations should not be subject to loosign the frequencies just because someone wants to set up a more powerful station in the neighborhood.

5. Microbroadcast pioneers, who created this moment by couragously committing civil disobedience, in the tradition of Ghandi and Martin Luther King, and for their pains have suffered government seizure and fines should receive amnesty, have their property returned, and be prioritized for new licenses.

6. Problems, technical or otherwise, should be referred to local voluntary micropower organization for assistance or mediation (as is done in the ham radio world). The FCC should be the forum of last resort.

7. LPFM must be included in the future of digital radio.

Thank you for your time and your consideration of these vital issues.

Sincerely,

Appendix C

EXCERPT FROM PHIL TYMON'S FIRST DRAFT OF CDC COMMENTS TO THE FCC'S PROPOSAL

INTRODUCTION

The Committee on Democratic Communications of the National Lawyers Guild (CDC) is very pleased that the FCC has initiated this rulemaking to establish a new low power FM (LPFM) radio service. We wholly support, in principle, the establishment of such a service. However, we are deeply concerned that certain elements of the proposal will lead to an LPFM service that does not succeed in addressing the primary needs that led to this rulemaking and may, in fact, simply replicate in miniature the current failures of full-power radio service.

The promise of a new LPFM service is that of:

• Local programming designed for local communities
• Diverse and alternative voices and viewpoints
• Service to currently unserved communities.

Current full-power radio has fallen victim to massive consolidation of ownership in a few hands; safe, bland, and homogenized programming designed for the lowest common denominator; and an abandonment of relevant local programming.

Since the advent of radio "broadcasting" in the 1920's, what was once a quite open marketplace of ideas and culture has slowly shrunk into a cramped and restricted corporate model. This corporate model has so pervaded our current consciousness that many are unable to see beyond it, to imagine an alternative form of radio broadcast communication. Yet it is really the corporate model that is bizarrely illogical, for it utilizes one of our main communications mediums not to communicate, but simply to amass audiences and sell them. Can anyone truly say that most current full-power commercial broadcasters are driven by an urgent desire to communicate? To communicate ideas, information, or artistic and cultural expression? Rather, they are simply driven by a desire to make money by selling audiences to advertisers. They might as well be selling shoes or tires or paper towels—its just a product to them, the content is interchangeable and basically unimportant.

The FCC has gone a good part of the way in envisioning a new type of radio service, an entirely new model. But we urge the FCC to go even further. It appears that a variety of goals and motivations underlie the FCC's current proposal. Some of those goals appear contradictory to us. As such, there is no coherent and cohesive theory that consistently underlies the FCC's proposal. We fear that the contradictions may eventually unravel the entire fabric of this new service and vitiate its dynamic ability to bring fresh, new, vibrant voices to American communities. Without a clear, consistent vision of what this new service should be, we believe there is a great risk that ten years down the road the small loopholes will have grown to freeways, and the same forces that have so enervated the creative spirit of current radio will dominate in LPFM.

Therefore, we propose that all decisions related to LPFM be measured by two guiding principles:

1. Encourage use of LPFM by those who have an urgent desire to communicate above all else—whether that be communication of information, ideas, art, or culture. Discourage those who wish to use LPFM as a means of making money.

2. Encourage maximum diversity of voices and viewpoints.

Wherever a decision needs to be made regarding implementation of LPFM these two principles should be applied.

We also note that application of Principle 1 is likely to significantly lessen the administrative problems that vex the FCC in this proceeding. If the new LPFM service is designed so that profitmaking is not a significant possibility, then we predict that the number of applicants will be greatly diminished. In addition, those who do apply will not be likely to invest great sums of money in attorneys and engineers to complicate and lengthen the process. Finally, those who are interested in applying will more likely be amenable to negotiated solutions, such as time-sharing, where there are conflicts.

We intend to refer to these two principles throughout our comments. We hope that the FCC will see the wisdom of applying such a coherent theory throughout.

AMNESTY FOR MICRORADIO PIONEERS

Prior to beginning our detailed analysis of the FCC's LPFM proposal, we must address an issue of overriding moral importance— that of amnesty for those who have steadfastly and bravely brought us to this point by consistently asserting their constitutional rights to free speech.

When Mbanna Kantako opened the modern microbroadcasting era in 1989 by transmitting local news and information to the mostly minority residents of his housing project in Springfield, Illinois the FCC could have responded by recognizing that a serious need was being addressed and asking how it could help to further Kantako's desire to support his community. After all, the FCC is supposed to work in the public's interest, is it not, rather than in the interests of entrenched broad-casting monopolists? Yet the FCC's reaction then, and for many years following, was simply to try to shut down such operations by whatever legal means possible. Had the FCC enforcement staff succeeded, we would not now be at this juncture.

The FCC initially dealt with Kantako as it had over the years with many unlicensed "pirate" broadcasters—assuming that an intimidating show of legal force would end the problem. But Kantako was the first of a new breed of unlicensed broadcaster. He was not a scampy, overenthusiastic teenager who wanted to play DJ,2 but a concerned citizen and community activist who des-perately wanted to do something for his community and was intensely frustrated by the complete neglect of the establishment media. He was not going to back down—he had been told that broadcasting was supposed to oper-ate in the public's interest, not solely to feed the greed of Mel Karmazin, Michael Eisner, Rupert Murdoch and a hoard of other corporate vultures who had clamped their mouths onto this "public" resource.

The story since then is well-known to the FCC. Rather than deter Mr. Kantako, the FCC's repressive pos-ture spawned a movement. A thousand transmitters bloomed in communities throughout the U.S. due to the overwhelming public need for a new kind of broadcast-ing and the courage of these pioneers. These unlicensed "microbroadcasters" were not criminals. They were not seeking to defraud the public, they were seeking to inform the public. They were not seeking to enrich themselves, just to enrich their communities. They had no criminal intent, motive, or purpose. Their purpose was to address clearly felt community needs that had been neglected and abandoned by both the FCC and the licensed broadcasters.

The FCC does not have clean hands in this matter.

It was the FCC's absurd notion that a government-created monopoly could be left to "market forces" for regulation that largely underlay the problem. The FCC's radio deregulation of the 1980s had done away with community ascertainment requirements, local programming and news and public affairs requirements, and commercial limits. But most importantly by making license renewal nearly automatic, the FCC effectively insulated broadcasters from any community input or influence. The ability of local citizens and community organizations to enter into a significant negotiating posture with local broadcasters in order to raise and address their concerns was eliminated. Broadcasters now need answer only to their absentee corporate masters.

It was also the FCC's enchantment with corporate visions of empire building that created the problem. The FCC long ago abandoned any vision of building and nurturing small, community oriented radio stations that were closely and keenly involved with their audience. Rather they continually pushed for higher power stations and multiple ownership both locally and nationally. No more mom and pops who lived and worked in the community. Stations were owned by large, faceless, distant corporations who piped in canned music via satellite and wired out the cash receipts to national banking centers. The FCC had completely lost the vision of radio as a means of truly communicating ideas and information among people and now saw it as simply a problem in engineering efficiency and cash flow production. The hollow men had triumphed.

As with any form of neglect and repression, there is a backlash. Short of open revolt, that backlash often takes the form of civil disobedience. Civil disobedience harms no one, it is nonviolent, it is not criminal, it is profoundly moral. Civil disobedience comes when people simply refuse to be bullied any further and assert the basic rights which are theirs, though they may have to assert them in the face of governmental force and repression. In the course of American history, those who engage in civil disobedience have nearly always been judged by history as morally justified. The government that had asserted its repressive force is nearly always condemned.

In 1954, Rosa Parks, despite legal prohibition, sat in a seat at the front of a bus in Montgomery, Alabama. Others sat at lunch counters, used drinking fountains, and entered public places and facilities that they were legally barred from utilizing. Would it not be odd, would it not indeed be perverse, if ultimately all African-Americans were given their basic right to sit anywhere in the bus they pleased, except for Rosa Parks? What would we think of the court or government that would say that she, and she alone, would forever be banished to the back of the bus because it was she, and she alone, who dared to confront the authority of the government, and who had, in fact, been the one to assert and win basic rights and basic dignity for all people? Such a result would be immoral, Kafkaesque, and laughable. Would you Chairman Kennard, Commissioner Ness, Commissioner Powell, Commissioner Furchtgott-Roth, Commissioner Tristani wish to be recorded in history as the ones who kept Rosa Parks sitting in the back of the bus? We urge you to think carefully about this decision. There are times to break free of the mind-numbing procedures and forms and language of bureaucracy. This is one of them. A stunted, bureaucratic retreat to the Commission's definition of "character qualifications" would ill-serve this proceeding and this nation. The pioneers who steadfastly brought us to this point have more than enough character to qualify as licensees. In fact, in our eyes, they should be given a licensing preference to reward them for their unselfish civic mindedness in the face of massive forces of opposition and even ridicule. The FCC must admit that this proceeding is occurring not out of the goodness of the government's heart, but solely because the unlicensed microbroadcasters have refused to back down, have refused to be silenced. Had they done what the FCC wanted, and turned off their transmitters upon receiving a warning letter, this proceeding would not exist.

We respectfully ask that the FCC act boldly, wipe the slate clean, grant an unconditional amnesty to all unlicensed microbroadcasters and start afresh. The pioneers of microradio must be given the opportunity to be "LPFM" broadcasters. Any other result would be immoral.

MICRORADIO CONTACTS

**NATIONAL LAWYERS GUILD COMMITTEE ON
DEMOCRATIC COMMUNICATIONS (CDC)**
The CDC is playing a major role in representing the community based micro radio movement and in mobilizing public opinion, and major progressive organizations in support of democratic, non commercial micro radio. For more information call Phil Tymon or Peter Franck (707.869.8270 or 415.381.9960) Email aakorn@igc.org. Web: www.nlgcdc.org.

THE MICRORADIO EMPOWERMENT COALITION
Advocating non-commercial legalization of microradio, the MEC is engaged in coalition building, public education, and lobbying. 2-12 Seaman Ave., # 5K, NYC 10034. Email: mec@tao.ca Contact through the New York Free Media Alliance: 212. 969. 8636.

NEW YORK FREE MEDIA ALLIANCE
NYFMA's web page archives many of the the legal papers and briefs filed by Robert Perry and Barbara Olshansky in Steal This Radio's lawsuit against the FCC. The site also features many other key microradio documents and links, including a photo essay of the October protest in DC, and other info from the free media movement: http://artcon.rutgers.edu/papertiger/nyfma Voice mail: 212. 969. 8636

RADIO 4 ALL
The grand nexus of microradio websites and activism information. Thanks to Lynn Gerry and Shawn Ewald, this site
weaves together microradio movement news, updates, legal
information, strategy, links, FCC rulemaking updates and
analysis, station contacts, technical primers, and information
about how to start your own station. An invaluable resource.
Check it out: http://radio4all.net

CENTER FOR CONSTITUTIONAL RIGHTS
CCR lawyers Robert Perry and Barbara Olshansky represent
Steal This Radio in its landmark constitutional challenge of the
FCC: *Free Speech vs. the FCC*. The Center is a non-profit legal
and educational organization dedicated to advancing and pro-
tecting the rights guaranteed by the United States Constitution
and the Universal Declaration of Human Rights, and to the creative use of law as a positive force for social change. Send for
their annual docket of court cases. 666 Broadway, 7th floor, NY,
NY 10012 Call: 212. 614. 6464 email: ccr@igc.apc.org

PROMETHEUS RADIO PROJECT
Borrowing its name from the mythological character who defied
the gods in order to share fire with humanity, the Prometheus
Radio Project defies the media industrial complex in order share
access to the airwaves with community groups in the East
Coast Area. Micropower radio referral, consultation, and advocacy. Call: 212. 946. 5251 email: prp@tao.ca Great website:
http://prometheus.tao.ca/

PAPER TIGER TELEVISION
Videos of microradio workshops, demos, press conferences, Subcommandante Marcos' video communique, and other subjects
that "smash the myths of the information industry." Activism
+ imagination + love = Paper Tiger. Send for their great cata-
log. 339 Lafayette, #6 NYC 10012 Call: 212. 420. 9045
http//:www.papertiger.org

GREG RUGGIERO